This is Me, Trying to Befriend Poetry

a collection of poems and rhymes

Ella Jane A. Pollero

Ukiyoto Publishing

All global publishing rights are held by

Ukiyoto Publishing

Published in 2024

Content Copyright © Ella Jane A. Pollero

ISBN 9789364946469

*All rights reserved.
No part of this publication may be reproduced,
transmitted, or stored in a retrieval system, in any form
by any means, electronic, mechanical, photocopying,
recording or otherwise, without the prior permission of
the publisher.*

The moral rights of the authors have been asserted.

*This book is sold subject to the condition that it shall not by
way of trade or otherwise, be lent, resold, hired out or
otherwise circulated, without the publisher's prior
consent, in any form of binding or cover other than that in
which it is published.*

www.ukiyoto.com

To my teenage self. We did it.

Contents

Darkness	1
I Longed for Heaven Though I didn't know What It Was	2
Every Silver Lining Has a Cloud	4
When?	6
He Should Have Said Otherwise	7
Pain & Girl: witness their show!	8
He Never Crossed the Line	9
I Am…	12
The Ghost of Tomorrow	13
Beauty	15
At the End of a Rainbow	16
Never Been a Star, Yet Twinkling	18
Wishing For Love	20
Are You at the Bottom?	21
Retell to the Blossom	22
I Would Like to Have Another Bite	23
Would You Like to Have Some Tea?	25
This is Me Saying…	26

Plea to Self	29
Please Stay	*30*
About the Author	*32*

Darkness

I Longed for Heaven Though I didn't know What It Was

(Sept. 16, 2020)

I wanted to reach the heavens
Heavens where angels reside
Reside with them and be in peace
Peace and ***tranquility*** solely for I.

I wanted to see the birds soar
Soar above the clouds as they fly
Fly to wherever they want to be
Be ***like them*** was longed by I.

I wanted to restrain my shackles
Shackles upon the ground that binds
Binds me for a whole lifetime
Lifetime to ***end*** was wished by I.

I wanted and longed to be free
Free of all the bucket of tears I cry
Cry from dusk till dawn and so
So **wasted** through death was I.

Every Silver Lining Has a Cloud

(Sept. 18, 2020)

cursed to be forever trapped
in the cold darkness doomed.
sight and point of view cursed
to see wilting before the bloom.

a tremble at the thought of the unknown,
a shiver despite the warmth of now,
looking at the glass being half-empty
and to risk being terrible somehow.

cursed to wallow in the shadows.
cursed to predict the bad side
rejecting hope and faith and light
like it was never wanted inside.

it's like something good wasn't yearned
while in fact, it has always been wished.
'cause somehow there's a part of the sight
knowing there are always shadows in the light.

When?

(Sept. 21, 2020)

A day when the sky is clear
And the minds of people are too.
A day when normal is like before
Not the now that the labeled new.
A day when everyone gets to run
Be wherever they want for fun.

Such a daydreamed day that is
Playing in our heads everyday
Such a distant day it seems
A day that's part of daily pray'rs
When would that day come?
Such a far-off fading hum.

He Should Have Said Otherwise

(Sept. 20, 2020)

I wonder why they have to spout lies
Then after that let out a sullen sigh
As if to prove to the ears and eyes
They only said empty words passing by.

No matter what kind of promises fly
The lows would never be the highs.
So, I'd rather have truths than be blind
At least I'm ready even as I cry.

"*Everything's going to be fine,*"
Was the statement of that guy
He should have added as he sighed,
"*It will be at the end of an infinite line.*"

Pain & Girl: witness their show!

(Sept. 25, 2020)

She stood; face neutral
A perfect doll-like maiden
Battered on the inside.
Controlled—

Like a puppet
With thin tight strings attached
Invisible to naked eyes—
By pain.

He Never Crossed the Line

(Oct. 15, 2020)

A kid so feeble and scantily clothed
Grew to know nothing but hurt and pain.
A kid so ignorant and naive and young
Knew nothing about loss and gain.
He only knew he was where he was,
And perhaps the beatings were the norm.
He knew not to be sad or angry or mad,
For he could not contrast right of any form.
The thrashing was a daily activity,
One he grew used to experience and have.
The curses were always heard and said
That he never once thought to be sad.

And it's scary and a pity for such a boy
For he never understood a thing.

10   This is Me, Trying to Befriend Poetry

He never knew what was normal or not
Until he had lost hope and everything.
The young boy, feeble and quiet as can be,
Learned of the outside of his walls.
There, by the street he cried and bawled,
The tears streaming like waterfalls.

He knew not what was bad from good,
And he knew not but to nod and endure.
He knew not what love was and the like
And he pitied himself behind the blur.

**"When you knew nothing
but one side of the coin,
You would never expect that there's
A better or worse half of what's going on…"**

he said, then whispered,

'…or maybe you would yet know it'll never come other than that of a miracle, or a curse.'

I Am...

(Oct. 17, 2020)

she was weak.
to fears she quivered,
turned and hid.
she was weak...

but she should have realized,
it's 'cause she said so.
you are what you say.
if you won't at least believe
you will never change.

The Ghost of Tomorrow

(Oct. 24, 2020)

I know of a frequent visitor
Late at night, when I'm alone.
A he, a she, an it, or a they,
I have no clue—it wasn't shown.

I'll settle for 'it'.

Its presence scares me—
A torture with no end.
Its visits I really hate—
But always, to its will, I bend.

I think I was hit.

Though, that's quite absurd.

This is Me, Trying to Befriend Poetry

How can it even be as such?
It's intangible you see,
Yet it pains me so, so much.

A monster it kinda fits.

When would I be not as scared?
When would I accept it's there?
When would I be able to resist?
The fright and the fear that I bear?

I mean, it doesn't exist yet!

Beauty

At the End of a Rainbow

(Sept. 23, 2020)

What can I find at the end of a rainbow?
What can I see if there I would go?
Is there a way to reserve the front row?
Is it really there as I stared by the meadow?

I've heard so many things that I could see
If ever at the end of the bow I would be:
Treasures and pots of gold and jewelry,
Or perhaps chocolates and treats like candy.

For a kid my age, about seven and a half,
These such things are fun things to have.
I even heard my friend with a pretend staff,
He'd be there and be rich—his mom laughed.

Others you see, like the mother of my friend
Do not believe a treasure exists at its end.
As for me, I don't know which way I'll bend
To believe or not to such sentiments.

But maybe it's because I wanted neither;
Not gold, or chocolates, or candies either.
The thing I want is not on the list of treasure
And so, I'm not sure if there I'll venture.

May I ask...

Is there a pot of liquid *laughter*,
Or a potion to make anyone *happier*?
Is there some kind of *stopper*
To the *shouters*, *screamers*,
beaters and *criers*?

At the of a seven-colored bow.
Would I find them if there I would go?

Never Been a Star, Yet Twinkling

(Sept. 20, 2020)

Mistaken for a star up high,
Named from the goddess of beauty
Well after all it is pretty.

Seeming to twinkle in the sky,
You'd never thought with one glance by
It's a planet you can then see—

Lucky Venus.

Not like those with a soundless cry
Once so bright, now dead—what a pity
Engulfing light, nothing is free
A blackhole—corpse—not seen in the sky.

Lucky Venus.

Wishing For Love

Are You at the Bottom?

(Sept. 24, 2020)

How can you utter such kind of words?
Such things that would make people fall?
Have you prepared a big hole?
'Cause it feels like you did.
With your every word
With every smile—
You being you—
I fall,
Hard.

Retell to the Blossom

(Oct. 03, 2020)

I tended to my own garden,
Watered the seedlings I've planted
Hoping they'd grow and they'd listen
To all the letters I've wasted.
If not an ear would hear me out
I would pour my words on flowers
And I will pray that as I shout
They won't wilt like my past lovers.

I Would Like to Have Another Bite

(Oct. 26, 2020)

Afternoon snacks are nice—a few drinks and a cake slice.

Afternoon tea is also nice if paired with crumpets and some pies.

I always loved the scrumptious smell that to my cravings I'd fell,

That I would leave a ringing bell for snacks the store would sell.

But maybe my favorite tea time is not worth more than a dime,

Just a little of your time as to my tea I'd drop a pinch of lime.

I just need a small bit of you—and your soul and heart too.

I just need a piece of you for my snack time to be not blue.

Didn't you know? A bite of your heart leaves a little show.

It's sweet and with a glow that makes joy in my veins flow.

It's the perfect paired snack for my tea time that so lacks.

I wish I could have a stack of your pieces reserved out back.

Yet I also know that your heart is one, the only one for someone,

And I wish that that someone is me and only me—the only one.

My teatime would be complete and I would never leave my seat.

If I would own the heart that beats, a heart that beats for me.

Would You Like to Have Some Tea?

(Oct. 13, 2020)

Brewed into the boiling stove,
Heated by the fire of strong will,
Freshly harvested herbs,
From the garden of words afloat.
Soaked in the gentle waters
There, by the brook of thoughts.
Slowly, earnestly made and prepared
With the pinch of desire to unfold.

Come and fill thy empty cup
And I'll ask you just once,

"Would you like to have some tea?"

This is Me Saying…

(Sept. 26, 2020)

This is me saying
Don't listen and hear
This is me saying
I wasn't here.
I'm not what I was
I'm not a lot of things
I'm not what you think
I'm not what I'm singing.

But there were you shouting,
You're calling my name,
There were you shouting
Taking your claim
That was you running,
Sprinting towards me

Coming closer and closer,
Till you're one foot away from me.

You said...

"This is me saying
I will always listen
I will hear your sobs
And I'm not mistaken.
You were right here
You were there for me,
And right now, I'm saying
You were what you couldn't see.
You may not be the tune
But you were the lyrics
You were the words
Hiding between the music.

And you were here
You will always be here

As will I
To wipe the tears
from your eyes."

... I didn't even notice that I cried.

Plea to Self

Please Stay

(Sept. 19, 2020)

Hold my hand and never let go.
Stay with me wherever I go.
Don't you dare leave and depart.
I won't last long if we're apart.

Tie a string around your wrist
Connected with mine so we won't miss.
Linked to the heart beating still.
If you're there, it'll always will.

Don't leave me on my own.
I won't last long all alone.
I'd be like an empty shell,
Easy to break if I fell

So…

Stay close to me.
Stay inside of me.
Stay with me—

Myself, don't abandon me.

"Everything's done once you've given up on yourself."

About the Author

Ella Jane A. Pollero

Ella is a college student majoring in Communication. She has been writing for most of her teenage years and has recently started dabbling in the arts under the name Blue on social media and *ao_hime* on Wattpad. During her free time, she enjoys drowning herself in books, movies, and anything with a story. She lives with her family in the Philippines along with a team of playful cats.

www.ingramcontent.com/pod-product-compliance
Lightning Source LLC
LaVergne TN
LVHW041641070526
838199LV00053B/3501